READ FOR JOY!

WRITTEN BY
CLAUDIA QUIGG

*Illustrations from various works by Tomie dePaola
used by arrangement with Penguin Putnam Books
for Young Readers, a division of Penguin Putnam Inc.
Cover illustration from Tomie dePaola's FAVORITE NURSERY TALES © 1986*

■

KATIE GROSS

BOOK SELECTION

■

SHARON JANKOWICZ

GRAPHIC DESIGN

AND

CALLIGRAPHY

■

For additional copies, contact
Baby TALK
Phone 217-475-2234 or toll-free 1-888-4BT-READ
ISBN 0-9674061-1-0 WEBSITE www.babytalk.org

COPYRIGHT © 2000

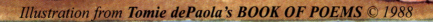

*Illustration from **Tomie dePaola's BOOK OF POEMS** © 1988*

READING ALOUD TO CHILDREN HELPS THEM IN SO MANY WAYS!

Reading together with your child is COZY. When you share a book, you enjoy being close. It is a time to give each other your undivided attention. This time says, "You are special to me!" Even after a bad day, reading together restores peace and love in the home.

■ Reading helps children learn about language. They learn new words and what they mean. Children hear words in books that they don't hear in conversation. The colorful pictures in children's books give meaning to the words.

■ Reading to children helps prepare them for school success. Hearing books read aloud helps children learn to listen. As they follow along, they learn that the "marks" on the pages have meaning. This gives them the background they need to learn to read. As you read for longer times, you help to increase their attention span. Being able to pay attention in school will help them succeed.

■ Reading to your children will give them new experiences. Your child can learn about a farm before he ever visits one! Pictures of cows, pigs and cornstalks can teach him what a farm is like. He can pretend to travel to the moon or the bottom of the ocean through books.

■ Books can prepare a child for her first visit to the dentist or her first day of school. Through books, children can learn about people who are different from the people they know. Reading about the unfamiliar can make it less scary. Books can expand your child's understanding of the whole world!

Quotations about reading are from Baby TALK parents enrolled in GED classes. In these quotes they share why they read to their children.

"I believe that if you read to kids, it encourages them to read when they get to the age where they can read."
-Sally

2

■ Sharing stories with your child can help him deal with problems. Does he think that no one likes him? Or that he'll never learn to write his name? Many characters in books feel that way, too. Reading about them may help.

■ Books help develop a child's imagination. Books teach her to think creatively. Listening to stories, she can imagine other possibilities for her own life.

■ Books make parenting easier. Once your child has learned to enjoy reading, books provide a fun activity. When you have to wait to see the doctor or sit still in the car, reading will make time pass quickly. Instead of becoming impatient, your child can wait happily.

■ But the best reason of all to share books with your child is this: Reading can be a joy! Books can be funny, amazing, sad, or inspiring. Illustrations in books are often great art. Books provide a time to forget your problems and relax. Enjoy this treat yourself. Raise your children with books!

Illustration from **Tomie dePaola's BOOK OF POEMS** © 1988

HOW CAN YOU TEACH YOUR CHILD TO LOVE BOOKS?

One way is by example. Let your child see you reading! When children see their parents reading, it teaches them that reading is important. Children who love to read come from families who read.

■ When you read something interesting, tell your child about it. He will learn that books are a good way to learn new things. When you read something that makes you laugh, share that with him, too. He will learn that books are funny. And when you read something that makes you sad, tell him about it. It will teach him that books have the power to touch real human beings.

■ Let your child know that you have favorite books. Handle these books gently to show that you value them. She will learn that the best books are to be treasured.

Illustration from **Tomie dePaola's BOOK OF POEMS** © 1988

HOW TO BEGIN READING ALOUD

When you begin to read aloud, prepare for success! Choose a time when your child is alert and happy. Make sure you turn off the TV and radio! Focus all your attention on your child. Hold her on your lap or sit close.

"When kids like their books, they learn not to write in them or tear them up. This helps them learn to appreciate things."
-Sally

■ Choose a book that you know will interest him. Start with something short. Talk about the cover and the pictures. Ask questions that will make him curious about the story. "Why is the boy sad?" or "Where is the dog hiding?" Asking questions will make him ready to listen.

MAKE READING ALOUD FUN!

When you read to your child, do it with enthusiasm! Read books you like. Use different voices for different characters. Read slowly to enjoy every word. Then read fast in the exciting parts! Make your voice sometimes soft and sometimes loud to add to the meaning.

■ Ask questions about the story as you go along. Your child will get more out of the book if you talk about it together. With older children, talk about the author and the illustrator. Ask your child why he thinks they made the book the way they did. He may want to read more books by the same author.

"When I read to my kids, they get excited. They point to the pictures. They can't wait for the next page."
-Cassandra

■ Find ways to bring the books you read to life. If you read BLUEBERRIES FOR SAL, eat blueberries. At bath time, read MAX'S BATH. When you read THE THREE BILLY GOATS GRUFF, act out the story. Take turns being the goats and the troll.

■ Watch your child's reaction. Give her a chance to see the illustrations. Answer her questions as you read. Talk about the pictures and the story. Be patient if she loses interest. You don't have to finish the whole book! You can put it aside to finish later. Never force a bored child to sit still and listen. Keep offering books in a positive way. She will learn that reading means special times with you. Soon your child will want to hear the whole story!

THE JOY BEGINS: READING TO INFANTS

*Illustration from **Tomie dePaola's** MOTHER GOOSE* © 1985

ROCK'N'RHYME

The best way to start reading to infants is not really reading at all! Babies like the rhythm of nursery rhymes. Their steady beat is comforting. Some people think that the rhythm reminds babies of mother's heartbeat. Babies love listening to parents chanting rhymes as they rock, walk or bounce.

■ Try to remember Mother Goose rhymes from your own childhood. Do you remember Humpty Dumpty, This Little Piggy, and Pat-a-cake? Say those rhymes to your baby from birth. She will enjoy them as millions of other babies have.

■ You can bring rhymes to life by acting them out. Help your baby clap as you say Pat-a-cake. Wiggle his toes as you do This Little Piggy. Soon he will expect this playtime from you, and will try to join in.

■ These are some of the best rhyming books. You can find them at your library:

ARNOLD LOBEL BOOK OF MOTHER GOOSE. Knopf, 1997. (revised ed.)

HAND RHYMES. Selected and illustrated by Marc Brown. Dutton, 1985. (also FINGER RHYMES, PLAY RHYMES.)

Lear, Edward. OWL AND THE PUSSYCAT. Putnam, 1991.

LUCY COUSINS BOOK OF NURSERY RHYMES. Dutton, 1999. (revised ed.)

MY VERY FIRST MOTHER GOOSE. Edited by Iona Opie, illustrated by Rosemary Wells. Candlewick, 1996.

NURSERY TREASURY: A COLLECTION OF BABY GAMES, RHYMES AND LULLABIES. Selected by Sally Emerson, illustrated by Moira and Colin MacLean. Doubleday, 1988.

PAT-A-CAKE AND OTHER PLAY RHYMES. Selected by Joanna Cole and Stephanie Calmenson, illustrated by Ala Tiegreen. Morrow, 1992.

TOMIE DEPAOLA'S MOTHER GOOSE. Putnam, 1985.

Illustration from **Tomie dePaola's FAVORITE NURSERY TALES** *© 1986*

THE EYES HAVE IT

READY TO LEARN

Babies spend a lot of time **staring** at things. As their vision develops, newborns like to look at contrasts. The pictures in many children's books have strong color contrasts. Your baby will enjoy gazing at them. Prop open a book with a bright illustration at the side of your baby's crib. He will enjoy the pictures!

 These books have bold illustrations which many babies enjoy:

Barton, Byron. MACHINES AT WORK. Crowell, 1987.
Crews, Donald. PARADE. Greenwillow, 1983.
Ehlert, Lois. FEATHERS FOR LUNCH. Harcourt, 1990.
Hoban, Tana. DOTS, SPOTS, SPECKLES AND STRIPES. Greenwillow, 1987.
Martin, Bill Jr. POLAR BEAR, POLAR BEAR, WHAT DO YOU HEAR? Illustrated by Eric Carle. Holt, 1991.
Williams, Vera B. MORE MORE MORE, SAID THE BABY. Greenwillow, 1990.

You will notice that your baby's attention changes through the day. Sometimes she is sleepy. Sometimes she is fussy. Sometimes she only wants to eat. But in every baby's day, there is some time when she is ready to look and listen. This is her "quiet, alert state." When your baby is quiet and alert, you can talk to her and she will look at your face. As the months pass, these times will grow longer. You can share books with her during these times.

Illustration from **Tomie dePaola's MOTHER GOOSE** © *1985*

SOME HANDY BOOKS

When your baby reaches about four months, he will begin to use his hands more. His eye-hand coordination will improve. First he will bat and swipe at things. Soon he will be able to grasp them. You will want to give him safe toys to handle at this time.

■ One toy he will enjoy playing with is a board book. These books have stiff pages which a baby can turn himself. Board books are sturdy and stand up to rough handling. He will first enjoy using the book as a hinge toy. Later he will study the pictures. He may show them to you and want you to talk about them.

"When you read to babies they recognize your voice. They use their eyes to make eye contact with you and to look at the pictures."
-Faye

■ Babies will enjoy discovering that pictures in books are always the same. They are learning that things still exist, even when they can not be seen. They are learning "object permanence." When they open a board book, they see the same pictures there each time. Pretty soon, they can predict what will happen when they open the book. They begin to feel that they can control a part of their world!

■ These board books seem to be favorites of many babies:

Barton, Byron. TRAINS. Harper, 1998.
Boynton, Sandra. BARNYARD DANCE.
    Workman, 1993.
Oxenbury, Helen. DRESSING. Dial, 1982. (also,
    TOM AND PIPPO books. Little Simon, 1998.)
Raffi. WHEELS ON THE BUS. Random, 1998.
UNDERSTANDING OPPOSITES. Playskool,
    1997.
Vulliamy, Clara. GOOD NIGHT, BABY.
    Candlewick, 1996.
Wells, Rosemary. MAX'S RIDE. Dial, 1979,
    1998.

■ Here are some wonderful Mother Goose board books:

Illustrated by Tomie dePaola:
    TOMIE'S LITTLE MOTHER GOOSE.
    Putnam, 1997.

Illustrated by Rosemary Wells:
    HUMPTY DUMPTY, LITTLE BOY BLUE,
    PUSSYCAT, PUSSYCAT, AND
    WEE WILLIE WINKIE. Candlewick, 1996.

Illustration from **Tomie dePaola's** *MOTHER GOOSE* © 1985

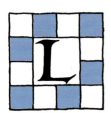 # LANGUAGE IN MOTION: READING TO TODDLERS

Parenting an active toddler can be a challenge! Reading books can make parenting easier in several ways:

■ Books give you something to do with toddlers as you wait. Waiting to see the doctor, waiting for a ride, waiting in traffic --- these times can be stressful with a two-year old! It helps if your child has learned to enjoy books. Always tuck a book in your bag. You will be prepared for waiting times.

■ When your child misbehaves, books can help him change course. If your toddler is in a bad mood, offer to read a favorite book. He may forget all about causing problems! He will enjoy this opportunity to start over as much as you will.

■ Reading can provide structure to a toddler's day. If she knows that you always read a book at nap time, she will expect that. She may stop fighting naps and accept them. She will look forward to special reading times through her day. This routine will help her feel secure. Young children need routines. Sharing books at regular times helps establish routines.

Illustration from **Tomie dePaola's FAVORITE NURSERY TALES** © *1986*

READERS ON THE RUN

A few toddlers will wait patiently as you read the words on the page. Most toddlers will listen for a moment, then move on to the next activity. This is normal. Many toddlers are too active to sit still and listen much. They are learning new motor skills. They may be more interested in walking, running, and climbing. When it comes to books, they may want to skip to the last page.

■ Read as much as your toddler wants to hear. Let your child set the pace for reading. Never force a busy toddler to sit while you finish reading a book! Many children are eighteen months or older before they listen to a whole book.

■ Keep presenting books in a fun, loving way. Soon toddlers learn that reading with parents is lots of fun. You will have helped your child learn to love books!

"No matter what time of day it is, when we sit down to read, my kids get peaceful."
-Andrew

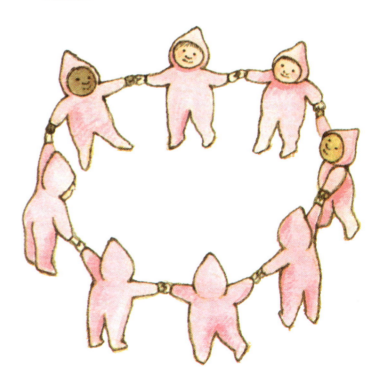

Illustration from **Tomie dePaola's MOTHER GOOSE** © 1985

OFF TO SLEEP: BEDTIME BOOKS

"Reading at night helps my kids go to sleep better."
-Faye

Many active toddlers have been put to bed happily with a bedtime story. It is easier to go to bed after settling down with a favorite book. Reading to your toddler at bedtime will encourage good bedtime habits. It will also bring a happy ending to the day.

■ These bedtime books have been enjoyed by many families:

Bang, Molly. TEN, NINE, EIGHT. Greenwillow, 1983.
Banks, Kate. AND IF THE MOON COULD TALK. Farrar, 1998.
Brown, Margaret Wise. GOODNIGHT MOON. Harper, 1947.
   (also LITTLE DONKEY CLOSE YOUR EYES. Harper, 1995.)
Ginsburg, Mirra. ASLEEP, ASLEEP. Greenwillow, 1992.
McMullan, Kate. IF YOU WERE MY BUNNY. Cartwheel, 1995.
Spinelli, Eileen. NAPTIME, LAPTIME. Cartwheel, 1995.

Illustration from **Tomie dePaola's BOOK OF POEMS** © 1988

WHAT IS IT?

Books are a good way to teach your toddler new words. This is one way that reading helps children develop language. As you read, point to an object on the page and say its name. Soon your child will want to point and name it, too. He will be proud to have mastered a new word!

■ Many books have been written with this very purpose in mind. Here are some excellent books for introducing new words:

Ahlberg, Janet and Allan. THE BABY'S CATALOGUE. Little, 1982.
Anholt, Catherine. BIG BOOK OF FAMILIES. Candlewick, 1998.
dePaola, Tomie. MICE SQUEAK, WE SPEAK. Putnam, 1997.
Hughes, Shirley. NURSERY COLLECTION. Lothrop, 1993. (revised ed.)
Ormerod, Jan. TO BABY WITH LOVE. Lothrop, 1994.
Priddy, Roger. BABY'S BOOK OF ANIMALS. DK, 1993.
Williams, Sue. I WENT WALKING. Harcourt, 1989.

"I think reading to kids helps them learn to recognize things---even things they've never seen except in books!"
-Sally

Illustration from **Tomie dePaola's FAVORITE NURSERY TALES** © *1986*

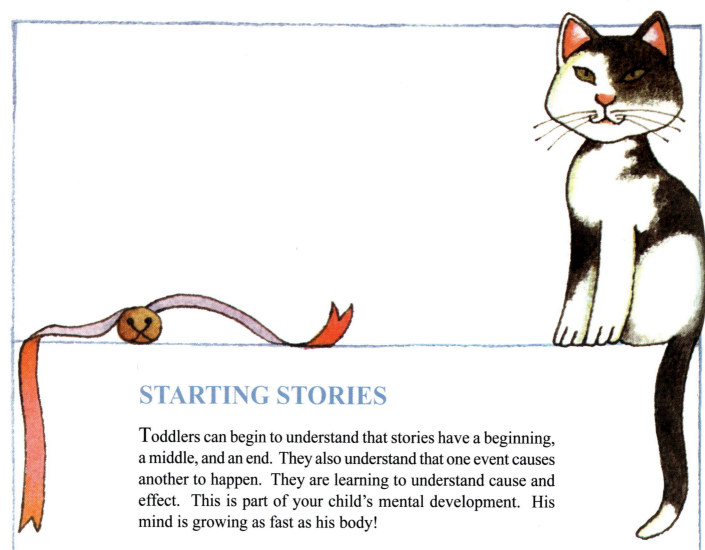

STARTING STORIES

Toddlers can begin to understand that stories have a beginning, a middle, and an end. They also understand that one event causes another to happen. They are learning to understand cause and effect. This is part of your child's mental development. His mind is growing as fast as his body!

■ As your child's mind grows, he will enjoy hearing simple stories. These stories set up a simple situation. Then, a problem occurs. In the end the problem is solved. Stories may teach your child how to solve some of his own problems!

■ Share these simple stories with your toddler:

Barton, Byron. THE THREE BEARS. Harper, 1991.
Burningham, John. MR. GUMPY'S OUTING. Holt, 1988.
Cooke, Trish. SO MUCH. Candlewick, 1997.
Lindgren, Barbro. SAM'S COOKIE. Morrow, 1982.
Rice, Eve. BENNY BAKES A CAKE. Greenwillow, 1993.
    (also SAM WHO NEVER FORGETS, 1977.)
Russo, Marisabina. THE LINE UP BOOK. Greenwillow, 1986.
Shaw, Nancy. SHEEP IN A SHOP. Houghton, 1991.
Simmons, Jane. COME ALONG, DAISY! Little, 1997.

Illustration from **Tomie dePaola's FAVORITE NURSERY TALES** © 1986

*Illustration from **Tomie dePaola's** FAVORITE NURSERY TALES* © 1986

PARTICIPATION BOOKS

As your child grows, books become very real to her. As you read a story, she will want to be actively involved in the book. Just as toddlers have learned to participate in life, they love to participate in books.

■ Many books invite children to participate. Some books ask questions. Others have flaps to lift or tabs to pull. A few books encourage children to poke, squeeze and sniff as they read.

■ Here are some participation books your toddler may enjoy:

Ahlberg, Janet and Allan. EACH PEACH PEAR PLUM. Viking, 1979.
Campbell, Rod. DEAR ZOO. Four Winds, 1982.
Cousins, Lucy. MAISY GOES TO BED. Little, 1990.
Crowther, Robert. MOST AMAZING HIDE-AND-SEEK ALPHABET BOOK. Candlewick, 1999.
Guarino, Deborah. IS YOUR MAMA A LLAMA? Scholastic, 1989.
Steig, William. TOBY, WHERE ARE YOU? Harper, 1997.
Zelinsky, Paul. THE WHEELS ON THE BUS. Dutton, 1990.

"When I read to my little girl, she gets out her doll and reads the book to the doll. My kids are learning to read by imitating me."
-Andrew

Illustration from **Tomie dePaola's BOOK OF POEMS** *© 1988*

READ IT AGAIN AND AGAIN

Most young children who love books have favorites. Sometimes a child will pick out one book to hear over and over. You may get tired of reading the same book. Some parents feel like hiding such a book so they won't have to read it!

■ Why would a child want to hear a book he has practically memorized? Maybe it makes him feel **smart** to know all the words. Maybe he likes keeping things the same. Or maybe he has connected with the book in a special way. That book has become a friend to him.

■ You should be happy when your child loves a certain book! You can be sure that he has learned that reading is a joy. Read it to him often, along with other books. Soon he will move on to new books. Thank goodness!

"When you read their favorite books, they catch you if you make a mistake or leave something out."
- Andrew

Illustration from **Tomie dePaola's MOTHER GOOSE** © 1985

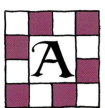# ACTIVE PARTICIPANTS: READING TO PRESCHOOLERS

THE CUDDLING CONTINUES

As preschoolers grow, they still need closeness and cuddling. Reading times help parents and children stay close. You can hold your preschooler while you read. It gives him an excuse to sit on your lap without seeming babyish. Books provide preschoolers with the quiet times they need in their busy lives.

■ While books offer security, they also help children grow. One way is by challenging them to grow in language and thinking skills. Preschoolers are able to enjoy more complicated picture books. These books have longer stories and more new words than toddler picture books. Preschoolers have longer attention spans than toddlers. They can listen longer. They can follow a longer, more complicated plot.

Illustration from **Tomie dePaola's FAVORITE NURSERY TALES** © 1986

SAY IT AGAIN

■ These picture books are beautifully illustrated and tell great stories:

Brown, Margaret Wise. THE RUNAWAY BUNNY. Harper, 1942.
Conrad, Pam. THE TUB PEOPLE. Harper, 1989.
Daly, Niki. NOT SO FAST, SONGOLOLO. Margaret McElderry, 1986.
Dorros, Arthur. ABUELA. Dutton, 1991.
Freeman, Don. CORDUROY. Viking, 1968.
Hughes, Shirley. ALL ABOUT ALFIE. Lothrop, 1997.
Hutchins, Pat. SILLY BILLY. Greenwillow, 1992.
Keats, Ezra Jack. WHISTLE FOR WILLIE. Viking, 1964.
McCloskey, Robert. MAKE WAY FOR DUCKLINGS. Viking, 1941.
Numeroff, Laura. IF YOU GIVE A MOUSE A COOKIE. Harper, 1985.
Sendak, Maurice. WHERE THE WILD THINGS ARE. Harper, 1963.

Preschool children love stories with repetition. Many books repeat the same words over and over again. Youngsters learn these lines, and enjoy saying them as you read. When you read "The Story of the Gingerbread Man," they will quickly learn this line: "Run, run, as fast as you can! You can't catch me! I'm the Gingerbread Man!" Being able to recite lines like these will make your child feel smart. Using books this way adds to your child's self-confidence.

■ Here are some books with repetition:

Carle, Eric. THE VERY HUNGRY CATERPILLAR. Philomel, 1981.
Christelow, Eileen. FIVE LITTLE MONKEYS JUMPING ON THE BED. Houghton Mifflin, 1989.
Ginsburg, Mirra. THE CHICK AND THE DUCKLING. Aladdin, 1988.
Emberley, Barbara. DRUMMER HOFF. Simon & Schuster, 1987.
Sendak, Maurice. PIERRE. Harper, 1962.
Slobodkina, Esphyr. CAPS FOR SALE. Harper, 1947.
THERE WAS AN OLD LADY WHO SWALLOWED A FLY. Illustrated by Simms Taback. Viking, 1997.
THE THREE BILLY GOATS GRUFF. Retold and illustrated by Paul Galdone. Houghton Mifflin, 1979. (also, THE GINGERBREAD BOY, 1983.)

"Reading to kids helps them remember things. Sometimes they memorize parts of favorite books."
- Sally

Illustration from **Tomie dePaola's BOOK OF POEMS** © 1988

READY OR NOT

Books can prepare children for new experiences. Books can help a child feel ready to try new things. Books can prepare your child for a new baby in the family, a visit to the dentist, or the first day of school. Children like to be ready for new experiences.

■ Prepare your child for new experiences with these books:

Barton, Byron. AIRPORT. Crowell, 1982.
Cutler, Jane. DARCY AND GRAN DON'T LIKE BABIES. Scholastic, 1993.
dePaola, Tomie. THE BABY SISTER. Putnam, 1996.
Henkes, Kevin. OWEN. Greenwillow, 1993.
Hest, Amy. BABY DUCK AND THE BAD EYEGLASSES. Candlewick, 1996.
Schwartz, Amy. ANNABELLE SWIFT, KINDERGARTNER. Watts, 1988.
Steig, William. DOCTOR DE SOTO. Farrar, 1982.

Illustration from **THE ART LESSON** *© 1989 by Tomie dePaola*

WHAT A CHARACTER!

Children often enjoy hearing several books about the same character. Characters in children's books make mistakes. They get their feelings hurt. Sometimes they are afraid. They may have problems to overcome. No wonder children identify with these characters! If your child likes one book from a series, try another. He may make a friend for life.

■ There are many fine character series for children. Try some of these:

Asch, Frank: the "BEAR" books
Bemelmans, Ludwig: the "MADELINE" books
Brown, Marc: the "ARTHUR" books
Brunhoff, Jean: the "BABAR" books
Hoban, Russell: the "FRANCES" books
Holabird, Katharine: the "ANGELINA BALLERINA" books
Hughes, Shirley: the "ALFIE" books
Kellogg, Steven: the "PINKERTON" books
Marshall, James: the "GEORGE AND MARTHA" books
McPhail, David: the "PIG PIG" books
Rey, H.A.: the "CURIOUS GEORGE" books
Stevenson, James: the "GRANDPA" books
Waber, Bernard: the "LYLE THE CROCODILE" books
Wells, Rosemary: the "MAX & RUBY" books

"Sometimes I notice my daughter acting like a character in a book we read." -Andrew

Illustration from **HAIRCUTS FOR THE WOOLSEYS** © 1989 by Tomie dePaola

HAPPY HOLIDAYS

Holidays can be a confusing time for young children. Adults are usually busy. Routines change. Sleep time may be disrupted. Children don't understand what all the excitement is about. They often react to holiday stress by misbehaving.

■ Books explain holidays to children in simple ways. These books explain the cultural or religious reasons for special days. Read to your child about holidays you celebrate. Also read about holidays that other families observe.

■ These holiday titles are great for older preschoolers:

Aoki, Hisako. SANTA'S FAVORITE STORY. Neugebauer Press, 1982.
Carlson, Nancy. HARRIET'S HALLOWEEN CANDY. Carolrhoda Books, 1982.
Clifton, Lucille. EVERETT ANDERSON'S CHRISTMAS COMING. Holt, 1991.
dePaola, Tomie. GET DRESSED, SANTA! Grosset & Dunlap, 1996.
Fishman, Cathy. ON HANUKKAH. Atheneum, 1998.
Hall, Zoe. IT'S PUMPKIN TIME. Blue Sky, 1994.
Hayes, Sarah. HAPPY CHRISTMAS, GEMMA. Lothrop, 1982.
Krensky, Stephen. HOW SANTA GOT HIS JOB. Simon & Schuster, 1998.
Paterson, Katherine. MARVIN'S BEST CHRISTMAS PRESENT EVER. Harper, 1997.
Pinkney, Andrea. SEVEN CANDLES FOR KWANZAA. Dial, 1993.
Waters, Kate. LION DANCER: ERNIE WAN'S CHINESE NEW YEAR. Scholastic, 1990.
Wells, Rosemary. MAX'S CHOCOLATE CHICKEN. Dial, 1989.
(also MAX'S CHRISTMAS, 1986.)

Illustration from **MY FIRST HALLOWEEN** © 1991 by Tomie dePaola

 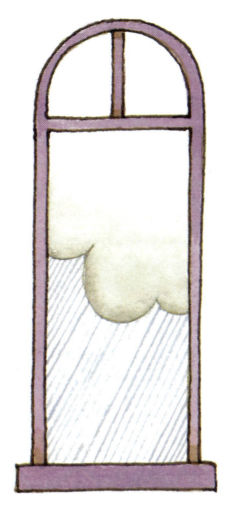 

BEYOND MOTHER GOOSE: POETRY FOR OLDER CHILDREN

The fun of rhythm and rhyme continues with poems for older children. Reading poetry to children is a pleasure. You may find yourself wanting to skip rope with a bouncy poem!

■ You may enjoy just one poem at each reading. Read the poem several times. After hearing it a few times, your child may be able to chime in with you.

■ Help your child memorize a short poem. It will build his memory skills. Poems learned in childhood are remembered for life!

■ These books are full of poems for you to enjoy with your child. Start using them now, and continue through his childhood:

PASS IT ON: AFRICAN AMERICAN POETRY FOR CHILDREN. Edited by Wade Hudson, illustrated by Floyd Cooper. Scholastic, 1993.

POEMS FOR THE VERY YOUNG. Edited by Michael Rosen, illustrated by Bob Graham. King Fisher, 1993.

Prelutsky, Jack. NEW KID ON THE BLOCK. Illustrated by James Stevenson. Greenwillow, 1984.

READ ALOUD RHYMES FOR THE VERY YOUNG. Selected by Jack Prelutsky, illustrated by Marc Brown. Knopf, 1986.

Silverstein, Shel. WHERE THE SIDEWALK ENDS. Harper, 1974.

SING A SONG OF POPCORN. Scholastic, 1988.

THE RANDOM HOUSE BOOK OF POETRY FOR CHILDREN. Selected by Jack Prelutsky, illustrated by Arnold Lobel. Random, 1983.

TOMIE DEPAOLA'S BOOK OF POEMS. Selected and illustrated by Tomie dePaola. Putnam, 1988.

Illustration from **Tomie dePaola's BOOK OF POEMS** © 1988

ENJOYING BOOKS TOGETHER: READING TO EARLY READERS

When a child goes to school, his world begins to grow beyond you. Continue to share books with him. It is a good way to stay close.

■ Don't stop reading to children who are learning to read themselves! Young readers still need to hear you read. Children can understand books that are too hard for them to read. For several more years, they enjoy hearing books that they can't read.

Hearing you read will help them learn to read better. They can follow along in a book as you read. They can listen to how your voice stops between sentences. They can hear how you read to give meaning to the words. Your child will listen carefully for tips to help him in his own reading.

■ Listening to you read interesting books will teach her why she should learn to read. She will want to read well enough to read those books. It will motivate her.

■ Listening to you read takes the pressure off of her. Many early readers feel pressure to read well. This can be frustrating! When you read to her, she can relax and enjoy the book. She will love books instead of fearing them.

FOLK TALES AND FABLES: CHILDREN'S NEED FOR JUSTICE

As children grow, they see and experience unfairness. Sometimes big kids pick on little kids. A child may get blamed for something he didn't do. Once in a while, bad things happen to good kids. These things can leave a child feeling mixed up.

■ Reading folk tales and fables may reassure your child. He will be comforted and encouraged because good wins in the end! These stories have appealed to readers through the ages. He will enjoy seeing the villain punished and the hero rewarded!

24   *Illustration from* **Tomie dePaola's FAVORITE NURSERY TALES** © 1986

■ Here are some great folk tales and fable books:

AESOP'S FABLES. Retold and illustrated by Fulvio Testa. Barron's, 1989.
ANDROCLES AND THE LION. Adapted and illus. by Janet Stevens. Holiday House, 1989.
BABA YAGA & THE WISE DOLL. Retold by Hiawyn Oram, illus. by Ruth Brown. Dutton, 1997.
BIMWILI AND THE ZIMWI. Retold by Verna Aardema, illus. by Susan Meddaugh. Dial, 1985.
GOLDILOCKS AND THE THREE BEARS. Retold and illus. by James Marshall. Dial, 1988.
IT COULD ALWAYS BE WORSE. Retold and illus. by Margot Zemach. Farrar, 1976.
JACK AND THE BEANSTALK. Retold and illus. by Steven Kellogg. Marrow, 1991.
JOHN HENRY. Retold by Julius Lester, illus. by Jerry Pinkney. Dial, 1994.
LON PO PO. Translated and illus. by Ed Young. Philomel, 1989.
THE MITTEN. Adapted and illus. by Jan Brett. Putnam, 1989.
RED RIDING HOOD. Retold and illus. by James Marshall. Dial, 1987.
RUMPELSTILTSKIN. Retold and illus. by Paul O. Zelinsky. Dutton, 1986.
SLEEPING BEAUTY. Retold and illus. by Trina S. Hyman. Little, 1977.
STREGA NONA. Retold and illus. by Tomie dePaola. Putnam, 1975.
TOADS AND DIAMONDS. Told by Charlotte Huck, illus. by Anita Lobel. Greenwillow, 1996.
TOMIE DEPAOLA'S FAVORITE NURSERY TALES. Putnam, 1986.
TOPS AND BOTTOMS. Adapted and illus. by Janet Stevens. Harcourt, 1995.

Illustration from **Tomie dePaola's BOOK OF POEMS** © 1988

PROBLEM SOLVING THROUGH BOOKS

Many books focus on characters who face problems. These problems may be like your child's problems. Is your child afraid of the dark? Is he the last one in the class to write his name? Is he terrible at baseball? Does he feel he has no friends?

■ These problems may sound small, but they are big to children! Children's authors respect children's feelings. They take the children's problems seriously. Your child may recognize herself in a character. She will see the character overcome the problem. She may get an idea about how to overcome her own problem. She will also learn something about solving problems in general.

■ These books feature characters who are overcoming problems:

Bottner, Barbara. BOOTSIE BARKER BITES. Putnam, 1992.
Bunting, Eve. FLY AWAY HOME. Clarion, 1991.
Carr, Jan. DARK DAY, LIGHT NIGHT. Hyperion, 1996.
Caseley, Judith. PRISCILLA TWICE. Greenwillow, 1995.
dePaola, Tomie. OLIVER BUTTON IS A SISSY. Harcourt, 1979.
Hazen, Barbara. TIGHT TIMES. Viking, 1979.
Henkes, Kevin. LILLY'S PURPLE PLASTIC PURSE. Greenwillow, 1991.
Jukes, Mavis. LIKE JAKE AND ME. Knopf, 1984.
Keller, Holly. HORACE. Greenwillow, 1991.
Polacco, Patricia. THUNDER CAKE. Putnam, 1990.
Rathmann, Peggy. RUBY THE COPYCAT. Scholastic, 1991.
Rosen, Michael. THIS IS OUR HOUSE. Candlewick, 1996.
Viorst, Judith. ALEXANDER AND THE TERRIBLE, HORRIBLE, NO GOOD, VERY BAD DAY. Atheneum, 1972.
Waber, Bernard. IRA SLEEPS OVER. Houghton Mifflin, 1972.
Walter, Mildred. MY MAMA NEEDS ME. Lothrop, 1983.
Zolotow, Charlotte. THE OLD DOG. Harper, 1995.

Illustration from **Tomie dePaola's BOOK OF POEMS** © 1988

WE READ TOGETHER: TAKING TURNS

One way to read with a new reader is by taking turns. Find an easy book. First you read a page. Then let your child read a page. Taking turns reading helps him get through books faster. He will stay interested longer hearing two different voices.

■ Enjoy listening to him read his pages. You can help him with words if he needs help. Be patient! Sometimes he will figure out a hard word if you give him time.

■ Most libraries have a section of books for early readers. Here are a few favorite easy-to-reads. Enjoy them with your new reader!

Byars, Betsy. MY BROTHER, ANT. Viking, 1996.
Lobel, Arnold. FROG AND TOAD TOGETHER. Harper, 1971.
Marshall, James. FOX ON THE JOB. Dial, 1988.
Minarik, Else. LITTLE BEAR. Harper, 1957.
Parish, Peggy. PLAY BALL, AMELIA BEDELIA. Harper. 1972.
Pilkey, Dav. A FRIEND FOR DRAGON. Orchard, 1991.
Rylant, Cynthia. HENRY AND MUDGE. Simon, 1996.
Seuss, Dr. GREEN EGGS AND HAM. Random, 1960.
Wiseman, Bernard. MORRIS AND BORIS. Dodd, 1974.

Illustration from **Tomie dePaola's BOOK OF POEMS** © 1988

A LITTLE EACH DAY: INTRODUCING CHAPTER BOOKS

Children enjoy listening to longer books with chapters before they are able to read them. Their attention span is longer now. They can remember a story from one day to the next. They look forward to hearing what happens next. Reading these books to them will s-t-r-e-t-c-h their attention spans. They will be able to follow more complex stories.

"Reading to kids calms them down. It helps them become good listeners."
-Sally

■ These chapter books are wonderful read-alouds:

Avi. POPPY. Orchard, 1995.
Cameron, Ann. THE STORIES JULIAN TELLS. Pantheon, 1981.
Cleary, Beverly. RAMONA THE PEST. Morrow, 1968.
Dahl, Roald. JAMES AND THE GIANT PEACH. Knopf, 1962.
Lindgren, Astrid. THE ADVENTURES OF PIPPI LONGSTOCKING. Viking, 1997.
Marshall, James. RATS ON THE ROOF. Dial, 1991.
TALES OF UNCLE REMUS: THE ADVENTURES OF BRER RABBIT. Told by Julius Lester. Dial, 1987.
White, E. B. CHARLOTTE'S WEB. Harper, 1952.
Wilder, Laura Ingalls. LITTLE HOUSE IN THE BIG WOODS. Harper, 1932.

Illustration from **Tomie dePaola's FAVORITE NURSERY TALES** © 1986

Illustration from **Tomie dePaola's FAVORITE NURSERY TALES** © 1986

PICTURE BOOKS FOR SCHOOL-AGE CHILDREN

Even after they learn to read, children still enjoy pictures. Illustrations bring a story to life and add meaning. Even adults may enjoy a good picture book.

■ Many picture books are written for older children. School children understand the humor or sadness in these books. Treat yourself and your child to these picture books for older children:

Ahlberg, Janet. THE JOLLY POSTMAN. Little, 1986.

Allard, Harry. MISS NELSON IS MISSING. Houghton, 1977.

Browne, Anthony. PIGGYBOOK. Knopf, 1986.

Cooney, Barbara. MISS RUMPHIUS. Viking, 1982.

Flournoy, Valerie. THE PATCHWORK QUILT. Dial, 1985.

Peet, Bill. BIG BAD BRUCE. Houghton, 1977.

Polacco, Patricia. CHICKEN SUNDAY. Philomel, 1992.

Rathmann, Peggy. OFFICER BUCKLE AND GLORIA. Putnam, 1995.

Say, Allen. GRANDFATHER'S JOURNEY. Houghton, 1993.

Scieszka, Jon. THE TRUE STORY OF THE THREE LITTLE PIGS. Viking, 1989.

Stanley, Diane. SAVING SWEETNESS. Putnam, 1986.

Steig, William. THE TOY BROTHER. Harper, 1996.

Van Allsburg, David. THE MYSTERIES OF HARRIS BURDICK. Houghton, 1984.

Wiesner, David. JUNE 29, 1999. Clarion, 1992.

Williams, Vera B. A CHAIR FOR MY MOTHER. Greenwillow, 1982.

Yashima, Taro. CROW BOY. Viking, 1955.

Ziefert, Harriet. A NEW COAT FOR ANNA. Knopf, 1986.

Illustration from **THE LEGEND OF THE INDIAN PAINTBRUSH** © 1988 Tomie dePaola

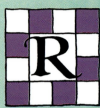

READING TOGETHER: SHARING BOOKS WITH OLDER CHILDREN

When they reach the upper grades, some children lose interest in books. You can help your child keep reading! This is a wonderful time for reading. Your child is able to read and understand so much more.

■ A good way to encourage reading and stay close to your child is to make reading a family affair!

Make it a household policy that everyone reads at bedtime. Tell your child that he must go to bed, but can stay awake and read for awhile. This will help your child calm down before sleep. It may also help start a lifelong reading habit.

Check out two copies of a book. You can read the same book as your child. Talk about the story as you read. It will provide for some great conversations.

Point out articles from newspapers or magazines which might interest your child. Many older children who won't read a book enjoy magazines.

Put a book and magazine rack in the bathroom. Kids who are "too busy" to read often find time in the bathroom!

■ Take a book along in the car or to the doctor's office. Your son or daughter will read if there's nothing else to do. This is a good way to use time spent waiting.

Talk about what you read at the dinner table or in the car. Let your child talk about what he has read. Read to your child while he washes the dishes, or do the dishes while he reads to you. Let him read to you while you drive.

Read aloud the first chapter of a book. This will spark your child's interest. She may want to read the rest by herself.

Let your child know how much you admire him for reading. Tell other people what a good reader he is. We all like to be praised! Hearing this will make him read more.

> "Older kids can read to little kids. It makes the little kids want to learn to read to be like the big kids."
> -Faye

Illustration from **Tomie dePaola's BOOK OF POEMS** © 1988

INFORMATION BOOKS

You can teach your child many things with books! He can learn about different kinds of people. He can see pictures of strange animals. He can hear about life in other countries. Books will help him learn that people are different and differences are good. This may help him to be an understanding person.

■ Books can be a source of new information. As your child grows, she will become interested in many things. Books about these topics will appeal to her. You can encourage her to read by finding books which will interest her.

■ Does she like dinosaurs? Does she collect rocks? Is she interested in flowers? Does she wonder where the sun goes at night? You can read together about these things.

■ Reading about school subjects will make your child a better student. Help him find books about other countries, or about famous people. It will enrich his learning.

■ Many excellent information books have been written for children. These are some of the best:

Anderson, Joan. COWBOYS: ROUNDUP ON AN AMERICAN RANCH. Scholastic, 1996.
Cole, Joanna. THE MAGIC SCHOOL BUS INSIDE THE HUMAN BODY. Scholastic, 1988. (and all the others in the series)
Jackson, Ellen. TURN OF THE CENTURY. Charlesbridge, 1998.
Lasky, Katherine. THE MOST BEAUTIFUL ROOF IN THE WORLD: EXPLORING THE RAINFOREST CANOPY. Harcourt, 1997.
Lauber, Patricia. HOW DINOSAURS CAME TO BE. Simon & Schuster, 1996.
Ride, Sally. THE THIRD PLANET: EXPLORING THE EARTH FROM SPACE. Crown, 1994.
Schwartz, David. HOW MUCH IS A MILLION? Lorthrop, 1985.
Simon, Seymour. LIGHTNING. Morrow, 1997.

Illustration from **Tomie dePaola's BOOK OF POEMS** © 1988

MYSTERIES: GOOD PRACTICE FOR PROBLEM SOLVERS

Many older children enjoy mysteries. These stories can be suspenseful. The scary parts in some of the books give children a safe thrill. Children can use problem solving skills to predict how the story will turn out.

■ Reading mysteries is a good way to learn why people act as they do. What motive might a thief have? Using clues, kids can begin to understand behavior.

■ Some mysteries allow children to choose an ending for the story. Others leave you wondering how the story will turn out! A good "who-done-it" is enjoyable for kids and parents, too. Many adults enjoy mysteries for their own pleasure reading.

■ Your library will contain many mysteries. Some are better than others. Here are some you and your child might enjoy:

Byars, Betsy. DISAPPEARING ACTS. Viking, 1998.
Corbett, Scott. THE LEMONADE TRICK. Little, 1960.
Lawrence, Iain. THE WRECKERS. Delacorte, 1998.
Newman, Robert. THE CASE OF THE BAKER STREET IRREGULAR. Atheneum, 1978.
Roberts, Willo. WHAT COULD GO WRONG? Atheneum, 1989.
Sobol, Donald. ENCYCLOPEDIA BROWN, BOY DETECTIVE. Dutton, 1963.
Stevenson, James. THE BONES IN THE CLIFF. Greenwillow, 1995.
Van Draanen, Wendelin. SAMMY KEYES AND THE HOTEL THIEF. Knopf, 1998.
Wright, Betty Ren. TOO MANY SECRETS. Scholastic, 1997.

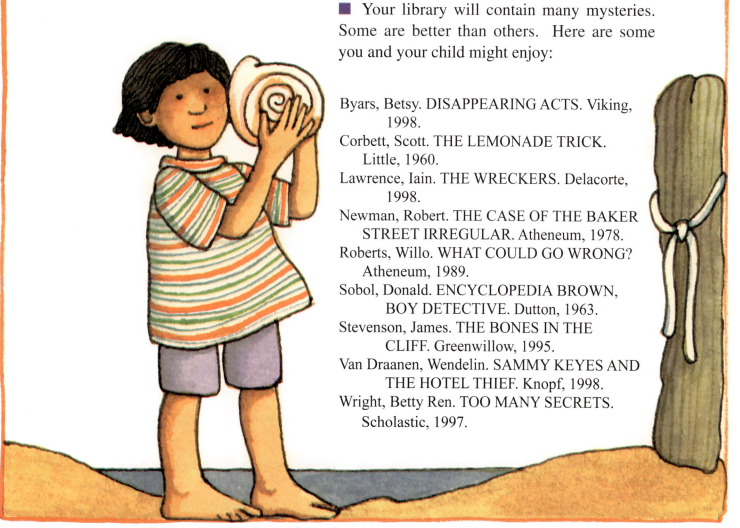

Illustration from **Tomie dePaola's BOOK OF POEMS** © 1988

FAMILY AND FRIENDS STORIES

As children reach the upper grades, their friends become more important to them. Many books written for this age group are about friendships. These books reflect the same hopes and hurts that your child may have. The characters experience many kinds of social situations.

■ These books explore many preteen social issues:

Cleary, Beverly. DEAR MR. HENSHAW. Morrow, 1983.
Clements, Andrew. FRINDLE. Simon, 1996.
Conly, Jane L. WHILE NO ONE WAS WATCHING. Holt, 1998.
Estes, Eleanor. THE HUNDRED DRESSES. Harcourt, 1944.
Hamilton, Virginia. COUSINS. Philomel, 1990.
Lowry, Lois. ANASTASIA KRUPNIK. Houghton, 1979.
Naylor, Phyllis. AGONY OF ALICE. Atheneum, 1985.
Spinelli, Jerry. MANIAC MAGEE. Little, 1990.
Williams, Vera. SCOOTER. Greenwillow, 1993.

Illustration from **Tomie dePaola's MOTHER GOOSE** © 1985

FANTASIES

Some books for older children are written about things that aren't real. Magical kingdoms and strange creatures exist in these stories. Characters may travel through time or have unusual abilities. These stories involve fantasy, and many children love them.

■ Fantasy books will expand your child's imagination. They give your child practice at thinking "what if...." Fantasies teach children to dream.

■ They also provide a healthy escape. In fantasies, characters experience great adventures. These adventures provide a change from everyday life. Children can imagine that they are visiting outer space instead of staying home.

■ Even though fantasy stories are not "true," they often contain important lessons. From them, your child can learn values which can be applied to her own life.

■ Try these fantasy books for a great escape:

Cooper, Susan. BOGGART. Margaret McElderry, 1993.
Du Bois, William Pene. THE TWENTY-ONE BALLOONS. Viking, 1947.
Jacques, Brian. REDWALL. Philomel, 1997.
King-Smith, Dick. BABE, THE GALLANT PIG. Crown, 1983.
L'Engle, Madeline. A WRINKLE IN TIME. Farrar, 1962.
Levine, Gail. ELLA ENCHANTED. Harper, 1997.
Lewis, C.S. THE LION, THE WITCH AND THE WARDROBE. Macmillan, 1950.
Norton, Mary. THE BORROWERS. Harcourt, 1952.
Pearce, Phillippa. TOM'S MIDNIGHT GARDEN. Harper, 1992.
Reid Banks, Lynne. THE INDIAN IN THE CUPBOARD. Doubleday, 1995.
Rowling, J.K. THE SORCERER'S STONE. Scholastic, 1998.
Selden, George. THE CRICKET IN TIME'S SQUARE. Farrar, 1960.

Illustration from **Tomie dePaola's BOOK OF POEMS** © 1988

BIOGRAPHIES: SOMEONE TO ADMIRE

Parents want their children to become great people. A good way to help is to provide role models. Many people have lived fascinating lives. Sometimes they have overcome terrible problems. Reading about such people is inspiring.

■ Don't you wish your child could meet Abraham Lincoln, Helen Keller, Martin Luther King, Jr. or Babe Ruth? Sadly, your child will never meet these people. But he can get to know them through books!

■ Biographies are books about people. If your child has a special interest, he can read a book about someone in that field. Does he love basketball? Give him a book about Michael Jordan. Does she want to be a reporter? She can read about Connie Chung. There are biographies about people from all walks of life, from the past and today.

■ By reading about people who succeed, your child will be inspired to succeed, and will learn how to do it. She will also learn respect for people who have made a difference.

■ These biographies are sure to inspire your reader:

Coles, Robert. THE STORY OF RUBY BRIDGES. Scholastic, 1995.
Cooney, Barbara. ELEANOR. Viking, 1996.
Dahl, Roald. BOY. Farrar, 1984.
Freedman, Russell. LINCOLN: A PHOTOBIOGRAPHY. Clarion, 1987.
Fritz, Jean. WHAT'S THE BIG IDEA, BEN FRANKLIN? Coward, 1976.
Krull, Kathleen. WILMA UNLIMITED. Harcourt, 1996.
Martin, Jacqueline. SNOWFLAKE BENTLEY. Houghton, 1998.
Parks, Rosa. I AM ROSA PARKS. Dial, 1997.
Peet, Bill. BILL PEET: AN AUTOBIOGRAPHY. Houghton, 1989.
Pinkney, Andrea. DUKE ELLINGTON: THE PIANO PRINCE AND HIS ORCHESTRA. Hyperion, 1998.
Sis, Peter. STARRY MESSENGER. Farrar, 1996.
Stanley, Diane. JOAN OF ARC. Morrow, 1998.

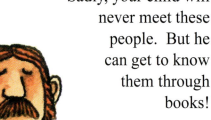

Illustration from **Tomie dePaola's BOOK OF POEMS** © 1988

GREAT LITERATURE: THE CLASSICS

When your child has learned to read well, he is ready for some truly great books. "The Classics" have stayed popular for many years because they are wonderful stories. These books are harder to read. They will "stretch" your child. But once he sinks his teeth into them, he won't let go. These are stories your son or daughter will never forget.

■ There are many versions of these classic stories which your child might enjoy:

Alcott, Louisa May. LITTLE WOMEN.
Baum, Frank. WIZARD OF OZ.
Burnett, Frances. THE SECRET GARDEN.
Carroll, Lewis. ALICE'S ADVENTURES IN WONDERLAND.
Kipling, Rudyard. THE JUNGLE BOOK.
Spyri, Johanna. HEIDI.
Stevenson, Robert Louis. KIDNAPPED and TREASURE ISLAND.
Twain, Mark. THE ADVENTURES OF TOM SAWYER.

■ These award winners could be tomorrow's classics:

Cushman, Karen. THE MIDWIFE'S APPRENTICE. Clarion, 1995.
Farmer, Nancy. A GIRL NAMED DISASTER. Orchard, 1996.
Fleischman, Sid. THE WHIPPING BOY. Greenwillow, 1986.
MacLachlan, Patricia. SARAH, PLAIN AND TALL. Harper, 1985.
Paulsen, Gary. HATCHET. Simon, 1987.
Speare, Elizabeth. THE WITCH OF BLACKBIRD POND. Houghton, 1958.
Taylor, Mildred. ROLL OF THUNDER, HEAR MY CRY. Dial, 1976.

Illustration from **Tomie dePaola's BOOK OF POEMS** © 1988

THE LIBRARY: YOUR FAMILY'S READING RESOURCE

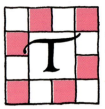

"Reading to kids makes you be a better reader, too!"
- Sally

Whether your child is six weeks old or sixteen years old, you will be welcomed at the library. There are books "just right" for every child and parent. The library is like a treasure chest of great books to read together.

■ Librarians enjoy helping children find books that will please them. Get to know your librarian. Let her know what your child likes. She will help you choose the best books for your child.

■ Make a habit of going to the library every week. This can be a family outing. Trips to the library are a way to have fun without spending money! These trips will teach your child that the library is a happy place.

■ Go to a library story time. Listen to the librarian presenting books. You can get ideas about how to read to children! Your child will enjoy story time with other children. Some libraries even offer "Lapsits" or storytimes for infants and toddlers and their parents.

■ Find out if your library has special reading programs. Many libraries offer rewards for children's reading. Help your child set reading goals. Celebrate as a family when he meets his goals.

■ Introduce your child to the library. You will open the door to a wider world, to the past and to the future. What better gift could you give your child?

Illustration from **Tomie dePaola's MOTHER GOOSE** © 1985